Animal Crackers

STACY SOFSCOLE

authorHOUSE®

AuthorHouse™
1663 Liberty Drive
Bloomington, IN 47403
www.authorhouse.com
Phone: 1-800-839-8640

First published by AuthorHouse   8/17/2010

ISBN: 978-1-4520-1056-4 (e)
ISBN: 978-1-4520-1054-0 (sc)
ISBN: 978-1-4520-1055-7 (hc)

Library of Congress Control Number: 2010910958

Printed in the United States of America

This book is printed on acid-free paper.

2: 27 Inspired Mindsoul
The wave of the New
And Everlasting Covenant:

The tide of the Old
Has resigned,
And now surfaces
The creature's creators Mind

For it alone
Gives the birth
Of moments time
Of the Earth

Animal Crackers

My uncontrollable thoughts
Despise my brain
I will be a victim no more

My throat it knots
Thirsts the same
My soul begins to roar

Eating away
Bite by bite
I find the inner core

Taste disgusts
Filled with puss
I find my chest is sore

Handsome Jack

I Will Not Build
A Tolerance of Brick
As I Cannot Co-exist
With AN Ignorant Dick

Urban silence/
Sleepless speak

Ground is wet
Silence rambles in its tongues
Falling asleep, not yet
Smoke filling the lungs

Street lights flicker,
In the airs moisture.
Heaviness of the city
Can't hold its own sidewalk.
Waiting for eternity is torture.
Tomorrow,
Why should it ever have to talk?

Night is calm, smirking.
Old wood creeks,
Expressing its monotonous exhaust.
Life is no longer smearing
Relax; the last drink has already been glossed.

Drunken masters
Have finished their lessons
All the doors have been locked
Last one to leave,
Enjoying every essence
Emptiness with me,
Free and wonderfully lost

Guiding Wildhearts

Don't try to catch a falling knife
Let it finish out its course
Let it work out its strife
Bounce about the floor
Wait for the feral spirits to settle
Flex its inner core
Pick it up, swipe it clean
Place it back in its drawer

Story of saving Grace

Tell me the story before it ends
Before it no longer depends

Tell me the story before it ends
Before it shrivels up and dies
Before darkness covers it with flies

Tell me the story
Of how the world ends
How we ate each others friends
How no selfness ever mends

Tell me the story! Tell me the story!
Please Grandpa, promise I won't worry
Really, really, it isn't that gory

Just tell me the story before it ends
Just before it no longer depends

Candy For Granted

Easter Morning's gay
Venerate the plough
Curse the World I may
Pigs excrete the cow

You can't control what isn't yours
Hormones deceive the conscience
Give yourself up to Mors
Throw your eggs
In the basket of defiance

Painters Progress

Lies remain the same
Hardest workers
Take the blame

Every layer always sticks
But Seeing-blind man gets his fix
- On coca-cola and barking orders
Even though he spills the mortar
On people who
Deserve the higher quarter

Seeing-blind man has no plan
But sleeps with a gun in his hand
- That shoots off at random
Into the eyes
Of the painters progress
Employed demise
Coat after coat
The painter tries

Lies remain the same
Hardest workers
Take the blame
As the horrid boss has no shame
For shooting off
With a blind man's aim

Existence?

Nourishing the infectious habit
Repugnant for a cause

Pondering life's collection
Fabric without a receipt

We have found the footprints
But argue the proprietor
Death will tell the truth

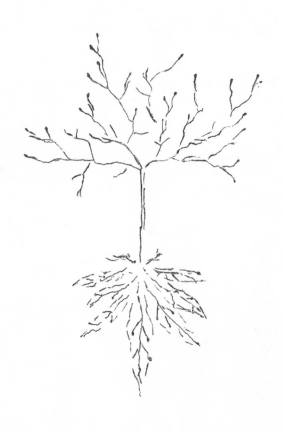

Tree

Up and down
We climb around

Within the trees
We scrape our knees

Bark it peels the skin away
Underneath the month of May

Corverb 7:29

Live life to the fullest
It continually fades away
Enjoy the fruitfulness
Of each and every day

Ooze

It is the gift
In which is wrapped
With softly managed elder sap

It is the thought
That can express
Your innermost soulfulness

It unaided moves the mind
Into uncharted depths
It can't unwind

Creativity is the key
That is distilled in you and me

Hormoan Garden

Flowers bloom
To early of noon
No one is left to see
The prettiness of innocence
Of what will never be

It is done
It has begun
The gift that keeps on giving
Dirty deeds will stain the sheets
Life will keep on living

Grand View Cleaners

Civilization's Social imbalance
Teetering on its useless talents

Ignominy and bigotry shouldn't entertain
Yet fill the mind with notions that stain

Society needs to be leveled
By true thought and spirit
Instead of the servile
Eternalized revel

Mind Kampf

Only way to fully grasp
Inner thoughts behind the wrath
Is to have lived
A life that has caused pain
From what of which the soul it drains

Once the glass has no more fill
Nothing soaks its empty spill
Leaving space for it to pour
Evilness into its core

Gormley Burble

Alyx and his Vorpal Snide
Whisping through the sleepless nighed
Kept on the cageless stride
'Till stagement struck him wide

He heard a sound Craver betold
About the bufools that turn to gold
From Gormley Burble of smoky mold
Everlas its vatients shold

Prickled smints went up his spine
Knowing not to mount this thine
Gimbled through his clotted mind
Slithed upon a work of kind

He too would also burble
Inquiring Gormley of his trouble
Retorting, "Why to think?
I have no stubble,
Just frivolsing the humble snuggle"

Sweesh aroma entranced Sir Alyx
Even Gormley's calm dynamics
Realizing their common standics
Alyx found him liking Frantix

Thus Sir Alyx found a friend
Gormley Burble of Redroot tend
Burbling naturally to comprehend
Cherriments of life it does lend

Alyx and his Vorpal Snide
Whisping through the sleepless nighed
Kept on the cageless stride
'Till stagement struck him wide

Cultural Baggage

Ignorance lives among us
It is something we can't escape
It lingers in the shadows
Explosively speaks its name

It exhausts the daily life
Of people who don't know better
False media is the knife
That slits quality character

Good Mourning to You

In the midst of our Darkness
I'll drink the water
Eat my flesh, Drink my blood
For you I give the slaughter
I must repent
For the sins I have not committed
My self loathing
Has not yet dwindled
Or expired
But I have forgotten to pay the meter

joy

You are my joy
That has removed my hazy Gray
You allow me to ploy
To keep my demons away

You are my cure
For my psychosomatic disease
My frankincense and myrrh
Honey from the bees

You allow me to live
A life free from dirty clot
You are so beautiful
Everything I am not

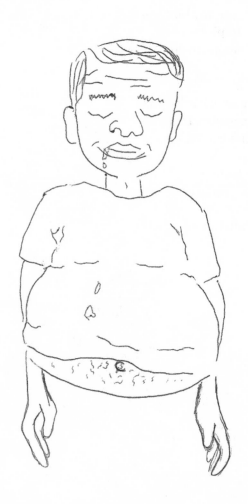

It's a Wonderful Death

Honesty stopped the feast
Living is a pain
Curiosity killed the beast
Life the bullous stain

Nothing goes untouched
Everything is wrong
Past is always clutched
Let's rejoice in song

Corverb 10:29

Give: respect, love,
And Honesty when needed,
Even though it has depleted

On the Hill

Season the Seasons
You just did beautiful

Now Stay focused On Staying focused
Distract distractions
So that we May begin the beginning
Of our new beginning

From apple tree
To grass
To ash
Burn and enlighten my judgment
Sweet Tree on the hill

Nursery Corral

Like a pick in a guitar
Or a straw pushed too far
Marriage to life
Keeps the keys in the car

We go where we want
We do what we like
Choosing to buckle with or without
While riding our bike

Prison cell
Maintains a long leash
Giving us room to spread our wings
Acknowledge our filthy feast

Emily's grasp of Satan's Sword

My white lie
Has gone black
Truth it hurts
My lips they crack

Spark me up
Another stack
Devils thirst
Has no track

Falling up
A soulful wave
Smoking love
On the cruelest day

"Tell all the truth
But tell it slant"
Tie it loose
Burn God's plant

Despotic

Guardians can even annoy
The Czar of irritation
Able to agitate nerves unknown
Make a simple day a complication

Forgive and quickly re-think
Reasons for their actions
They try but can't deny
Their loss of juvenile passions

One Way →

Road narrows
Lane ends
Merge

Soft shoulder
Now a low shoulder

No detour
No U-Turn

25 miles per hour
Now 45

Keep right
Road Work Ahead

Elevation quickly rising
Chains required

I hope this isn't the wrong way

Ash Land

Life is forever
So let us waste it

No tragedy from war
So let us wage it

Death is not here
So let us fear

- Our sweet compassion
And Cheeking tear

Carriage Way

My good fortune keeps an eye
Yet wants to sting me

I just dislike people in general
Most do not stand
They fear the needless
Self-serving interests

Burns my Judas fuel
This Propsoul standard

Devil's eyes
Are in the sty of the beholder

My smile brings discomfort
To All those who apply

Darkest Night

Borne Pathogens
From tongue to ear
Complete separation
Never felt so near

Casualty Station
- Platform Pariah
Life's realization
That we all die a –

Lone

But we find our true friends
In an empty room we never knew

NerdRum/Into Void

Clicking clocks
Ticking talks
Past time comes to follow
Photo stills the hardening hollow

Offending faucets
Mirror affects
Moments mount itself and rest

Tending toys
Painting brain
Further employs
Its canvas name

Corverb 11:11

Reality always has its levels
Sometimes
You have to take the stairs

Piece of Mind

Puzzling her missing pieces
In and out of order
Resolving her mental thesis
Starting from the border

Referring to the box
Finding the picture in her head
Unlocking all the locks
That confines her thinking thread

Disassembled absent links
Assorting all the seasons
Straightening out all the kinks
It is the time of reason

Comatose

Its mind is lending you sounds
Of adolescent lethal rounds
Forbidden lewd events
Establish our untitled contents
Properly regarding our affairs
Assuming siblings
Should never be shared

Little Trees

Oh Grand Oak...

Nourish the depths
Of the infallible mind
Expand your lungs and breathe
Bring home human kind
Advance your easy breeze

Purity cleanses the conscience
Enriching the verve in its whirl
Forever falls your natural rinse
In this congested coagulating world

Monday

Ingrate strikes again
- Remorse was not provoked

Why can't I feel?

Hollowness brings laughter
Fury ensues
It can't handle silence
Playing mind games
- Clockwise, it's your turn

… Hello Tomorrow
No signs of tremors
No wreckage to be found
Clean from sullied recollections
Wiped from past thoughts

So sweet and So sound?

Cracking Walnuts

Look above
Not ahead
Realize how small you are

Come to
Visit your senses
Have a slice of the humble sky

Nothing creates nothing
Thus we are here
Treat your brother well
Forget to regret our queer position

drawroF

There is nothing more
Life is done
The world has left
There is no more sun

Light it fades
Redeem the Lord
Mankind destroyed
We choked the cord

Intermission …

… With best intentions
Concepts varied
Humans came
With wisdom buried

God has come
Among us Men
Speaks the word
He walks again

Jesus lives
Still it burned
Species' thrived
Earth it turned

It all began.

parenting Children

Absorbed calamity
Elders used and abused
- At the owners expense

Punishment, lack there of
You have to be good to be bad
Practice makes perdition

Kill them while their young
Help us keep our sanity
Our ideals of a future family

Happy Birthday

I know the gift card
Says it's for $20
But it really
Only has $13.75 on it.
So why don't you spend it wisely,
You mumbling, fumbling buffoon.

Love,

Desmond

Filling an Empty Throne

B: In darkness you feel
What's the point of living?
It all ends the same
There's no use in crying
When your soul's ashamed

Reality takes its course
When you don't feel any remorse
For all the people who don't care
All the people unaware
Of your situation

A: The point of living
Is that it all isn't the same
Only Use in crying
Is when there's no one to blame

Remember that
Not all people care
Not everything is fair
Just show them joy
Allow them to share

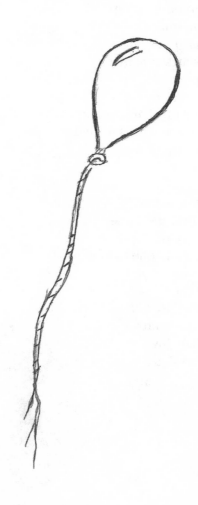

Oh Joe

A foolish being once verbalized,

"Life is hardest test
You'll ever take
Hence, be consumed by your study
Don't make a mistake."

The wise man then realized
That he had not lived

Corverb 1:27

Wisdom comes with experience
Not with age
The ones who shorten tall
Construct the stage
That gives us all
Space to relieve our cage

The American Seeker

Swallow your smoke
Letting it do its grime
Sport shades in the shade
Hiding your black eye, you say
When they are really pink

Feel your beating heart
But don't panic
I saw the light was on
So I came in
I hope you don't mind
While I fertilize
- The flowering American Seeker

Inundate the conscience
Substitute the drivel days
- With wits of the milieu
Have them fall and stick
Like Velcro onto a carpet skull

Sustain a student of the surge
Recall that death is faithful
Web beyond
Before a long way gets behind

Brownish

Here I am left alone
Everybody else has company
No one of comfort to call my own
Since Tuesdays and Thursdays
Are with Morrie

Relief of pressure can be freeing
Only temporarily for awhile
Though masturbation sooths my teething
Happiness can only come
With a sharing smile

Queen Duck

Painting the roses blue
For what reason?
It's not what I wanted to do
But she says "it's the season…

…for coloring the ocean medium"
Even though it will never dry
Rescue me out of my tedium
I'd rather be poor and dye

It's not the fact that I am stuck
But the constant bicker I get
Quacking of Donald Duck
Up and down my neck
About the things I never met

Time for Worship

God is a scientist
Satan, his janitor

Creating a test
That dwells in his monitor

Lucifer cleans up the mess
Receives all the trash

God, our Father
Satan, The Milkman

Designed against our placement
To saw off our horns

We are born in sin
But expected to deliver

Mother Earth our whore
We Bastards mistreat her

Dear Prudence,

My regards are focused on your well-being and current location. This past visit did not seem long and I worry about your safety. I have not heard any news of your health and it invokes concern. This lack of knowledge only plagues my mind in your continuing absence. I truly hope that you should receive my reverence and respond, to fill my empty unawareness.

Earnestly,

Your Friend

Post Script
Please come home

Once, Again

Aches of your cry
Shrink my heart

Tears do not suit you well

Flushing guilt
Tears my soul
Knowing I have no control

Descent into my open fortitude
Nestle in my oven-warm Ardour sheath
Never fear what is underneath

Corporate Reign
Window Pain

Water Drops
Gathers its suspended neighbors

Water falls
Leisurely beginning
Rushing to find its end

Water drops
Roaming, to designate its path
Growing, relying on its mass
Furthering its unavailing task

Water falls
As everything does
Concluding abrupt
As it never was

Water drops
Holding its mark on the window pane
Until the next acerbic shower of reign

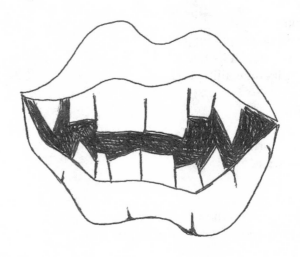

Inane Drone

Can't exorcize their mind
If they don't have one
It's not kind
To pretend

Wasted time
If you don't have none
You can't shine
It don't lend

Go outside
Try to find some
If not fine
Do not tend

Since you're dead living
You have no meaning
Your futile bones
Stop their quivering

Corverb 4:20; 4

Please hate
I will disregard
Your emptiness will remain

Hogwash

Damn the Raths
All their regulations
Go save some lives
Instead of wasting patience

Some have probable cause
But for the ones who don't
Their short-man complex gnaws
Eating at the throat

Stop wasting our money
Go get some self-esteem
Stop raining when it's sunny
While you fulfill your faggoteer dream

93

Life Savor

Don't break me up
Take me all at once and savor
My lover I will forget
Remember my lasting flavor

New Years

In the middle between old and new
Passion filled to the rim
In the middle between me and you
Overflowing Midnight swim

Feather-soft silky skin
Laid across the leather seat
Honey spout milking sin
Splicing spirits, conversing feet

Underneath the citrus moon
Open spores drip the salt
Of sonic waves meeting dunes
Coming to its gentle halt

Weather Man

Stop the rain
Don't push me away
Let me join in
I'll bring the sun to play

Can't shelter the storm
When it's blowing the town
Come, allow me to warm
Turn your frown upside down

Know no worries, feel no pain
Snuggles and cuddles,
Jumping in puddles
Just singing in the rain

In Search of A "Lighter"

I didn't know where I was
So I started over

Had a full-service fluid change
I don't know the same

I was to expect the expecting
But it by no means came

It just takes some time, maybe
Evaluate and re-assess
Take it all in, stop
Wait to come up to the surface
Buoyant and out of breathe

Cultivating Frozen Yogurt

She's laughing at us
Rather stalwartly
With her creamy milk mustache
Chewing over our appearance

She's laughing at us
Benefiting from her undisturbed print
Protected by irresponsibility
Having a giggle

She is darling
Unacquainted with good, bad and evil
Topped–off with Cherub charm

She is darling
Just icing on the cake
In an otherwise soft-served position

Apple on the orange tree

An Amalgamated soul
Has been shunned
Under the strict control
Of a misinformed nun

Who is she to say?
What is wrong to thee?
Just natures gift
As an apple on an orange tree

Simply a Berdache set free

Corverb 12:2

As For the nun herself;
She is a nice man.

Departure's Arrival

When she speaks
Her bottom lip greets
- Her elongated Yellow picket fence
While struggling
To keep her mouth closed

Open wide
You can't control the shove,
But defend
You're a poor educated educator
Having to put up with the critics
Of a second class

Just spit it out of your mouth
Cleanse the integrity
Of your profession
So that I might get on with my day
In a calm state of flight

Life: Act 2 Stage 6

Enjoy the basking in the sun
Feel the numbing of my eyes
Hope the climax never comes
In this constant climb

My peak will be the end of me
I'll make sure it never happens
Until I sense a new play
Starring Iggy Pop and Charlie Chaplin

Wooden Boy

Just like in the movies
Picture perfect

A Living lie
That has become more than a friend

Acting is reacting
Playing along

How far shall he go?
Before he has no more
- Room to remember his placements

- Of time, crime, nickel and dime
Now shame

Extract

Custom thoughts Subject to change,
When driving through purgatory.

Plant them in gypsum soil
Let them run

- Free range

St. Patty's Day

You are done dripping
It is all over
A duet turns into a monologue

Driving snakes out of my mind
With my thick staff
Filled with memories
Never to return

No more qualms
I am owner of my own

No more misinterpretations
- Between the virgins no more

Time/energy swept away
Friends? Well acquaintances

Propsoul Brand

Vacant bodies
Echoing the current
Programmed machines
Respond So Fluent

Deflecting to protect
Their invalid worth
Artificial living
Forging their Mirth

Acting surprised
Bluffing naturally
Awe in Vainglorious
Blind vision reality

Alter your ego
Before your death has no value

God's Fruit

Her noble coul
Has left her in a social cocoon
Collecting a Sterile towel
To wrap around the fruit of the womb

Beyond the walls of depth
Lay her Building blocks inside
Where secret thoughts are kept
Where she will run and have them hide

She will learn to hush and live
Observing every eye
Creating abodes in her head
To help her learn to fly

Aging is not the problem
It is getting old
For There will come a time
When she will have to make her mold

But for now she is fine
Her noble coul
Has left her in a social cocoon
Collecting a Sterile towel
To wrap around the fruit of the womb

Community lesson

Before you hit the first key
You need to format.
Confess your confusion
Agree -
On Your particular convention of truth
Then wait to waste your time arguing.

Corverb 9: 11

Time is fleeting
In this slow death called life
Stay calm, just follow
Remember – "Status Quo"

Solo Interview: Arsonist

I Smoke Out the bugs
That Aggravate
Where my conscience dwells

Ignited my Zippo
Teacher caught me burning
- Orbital rings of pungent reflections
I deny the fumes

"Class, Think before you act.
Everything has a consequence"
Yeah, I know
"Having who ever arrested for arson"
Yeah, Not me

Just a Social exercise
Foaming at the mouth
I have no control
Blameless? I am to blame the flame
Calm down there is no evidence

Although On the floor
I see dead cockroaches

Looking Into the Sun

Virgin of the Reyes
Amaze the days
With the simple haze of Grace

Glory never fades
It always stays in place
As long as you're eager
To continue your ever graze

Light seeks Good
While Good seeks Glory
Grace is chaste pleasure
That's the morale of the story

Manette: a bore

Swinish multitude
Became callow spoiled meat
While fecal matter brewed
High above the feet

They talk about the other sex
As if they were a steak
A meaty empty object
That they will never take

It is Impossible for them to suppress
Their Indolent snorting eagerness
To find their slaughter seat
Waiting for Packaging to be complete

Putting soiled pigs into the grind
Providing that
The Gospel of the sweetened swine
Permeates through the blackened mind

Head Gears

Midnight oils
My rusty muse
Weakness coils
While I take out my tools

My turning screw
Is now stripped
Replacing a new
With fine grip

Cranking, Tuning
Tightening the strings
Placing, Refueling
My Creative springs

It is now time
For me to rest
My body to unwind
While my head makes another mess

NovaCane

Master pilot
Of the mental plane
Opening curtains
To a higher ground
Cropping NovaCane

In the sky tube
We hold no shrine
Sharing the road
Within in a Masterpiece Theatre
Bouncing on cloud 9

Stainless environment
We hold no shame
Opening windows
To a good draft
Harvesting NovaCane

Rainbow End Finders

Don't let the Giants stop you
From seeing the end
Over power them
They'll bow to your pen

Ride on their back
Allow the native to return
Destroy the old stock
- An Auto-Man Empire
Watch it burn

Create compost
Drop rich seed
Slab a foundation
Build quarters of good men
- A population aficionado
There you will find your Rainbows end

Love Letters from the Devil

Let's rekindle our disgust
Start where we left off
Let's runaway together
To a Paradise Lost

I beg you to follow
Join me in my coming
Taste my dirty prescription
As your pain yields to numbing

Live in suspended animation
In a summer of discontent
My South Sector Province
Imagineering dire portent

I know Father doesn't like me
Sneak out the gates
Kill your mother she deems-
We are false fated Soul mates

Killing a ladybug

Accidentally on purpose
There was no cause
- In chinking the chain.
I stepped right on her
Out of instinct and reaction

Within in the lost emotion of disgust
Which I did not mean to find

What is there no to like?
Even if she wasn't a lady
But she was

As I reflect and quickly regret
My mindless act
Please forgive me
I have learned my lesson
I will see again

Corverb 3:10

Process, take your time
After all it's yours not mine.

Mother Mar & the Dead Fish

She offers me everything
Amongst the ocean spray
Cold saltwater warms my skin
No need for shore
When the sky is grey

Her rapid wash combs my hair
As I bob along
Gifts of driftwood float by
Sandfeet sink
Listening to her song

Tickling my soul
As I pierce thru her waves
A fetus boundless
In Utero
Embracing a Mother's prays

Sidewalk Mocking

Eating sidewalk is always fun
Losing teeth, breaking jaw,
Looking down the barrel of a gun
Well, that's just the fun of it all

But yesterday you had your turn
I was just walking along
And felt a burn
I looked down only to see
You ate a hole out of my sole
Now I can hardly be

Dumbfound Me

We are all looking
For something
But we don't know what

We all want company and truth
But we rarely find
Truth in company

We all want to be productive
But we more often than not
Are driven to be productive solely
For our recreation

If you look closely people
Have all gone crazy
But have learned to (somewhat)
Keep composure

And for the people
Who barely show crazy
They have just learned
To believe their lie

They all try to forget what they really want
Or maybe they have just given up
Either way they sidetrack their focus
Into a system they don't
Fully understand

But at the end of the day
It doesn't matter
There's food on their plate
And some change in their pocket
Just enough to buy tomorrows meal

It doesn't matter if you are
At the bottom or the top
Your still part of the system
The machine that steals
Your life and time before your eyes

Why don't we ask each other?
Why don't we come together?
Why don't we drop the bullshit
Out of our left hand
And clean it with our right?
Why don't we get something done
Before we kill each other?

We all talk, but why?
Action is louder is than words
I guess I don't understand

Is everybody dumb or just me

Retiring faith

What's going down sunshine?
I've been chasing you all day
Failure to notice the use of my head
Are you playing attention?
I Work hard to keep my amusement

Taxing the Terrestrial enterprise
Fasten your seat belts
Suspended animation begins
Wait, you didn't put your Mask on

Dispose of Practical Energy

Squeezing the lime
Got whet on his whip
Gods gift to the natives
Sticks to his lip

He know not why
He just goes through his day
Walking in a haze
To make is pain go away

Although he feels
That his just buying time
His actually wasting it

Dispose your mind
Or the Receptacle
Will make it disposable

I'm Running out of Ink

I don't know any more words

Corverb 8:0

When you're finished changing
You're finished
Yet I will continue my
Perpetual Harmony

Printed in the USA
CPSIA information can be obtained
at www.ICGtesting.com
CBHW030923121023
1234CB00003B/2/J